Brush With Greatness

Leonardo da Vinci

Michael DeMocker

PURPLE TOAD
PUBLISHING

Copyright © 2017 by Purple Toad Publishing, Inc. All rights reserved. No part of this book may be reproduced without written permission from the publisher. Printed and bound in the United States of America.

Printing   1   2   3   4   5   6   7   8   9

Goya
Leonardo da Vinci
Michelangelo
Monet
Van Gogh

Publisher's Cataloging-in-Publication Data
DeMocker, Michael.
   Leonardo da Vinci / written by Michael DeMocker.
      p. cm.
Includes bibliographic references, glossary, and index.
ISBN 9781624691935
1. Leonardo, da Vinci, 1452-1519—Juvenile literature. 2. Artists—Italy—Biography—Juvenile literature. I. Series: Brush with greatness.
  N6923.L33 2017
  709.2

Library of Congress Control Number: 2016937168

eBook ISBN: 9781624691942

ABOUT THE AUTHOR: Despite being a dashingly handsome, globe-trotting, award-winning photojournalist, travel writer, and Renaissance Man based in New Orleans, Michael DeMocker is, in truth, really quite dull, a terrible dancer, and a frequent source of embarrassment to his wife, son, and three dogs. He does speak passable Italian, however.

Contents

Chapter 1
Learning to Fly 5

Chapter 2
The Master's Workshop 9

Chapter 3
The Young Genius 15

Chapter 4
The Milan Years 19

Chapter 5
My Stepmother, Lisa 23

Timeline 28

Selected Works 29

Further Reading 30

Glossary 31

Index 32

Giotto's campanile, or bell tower, rises 277 feet above the Italian city of Florence.

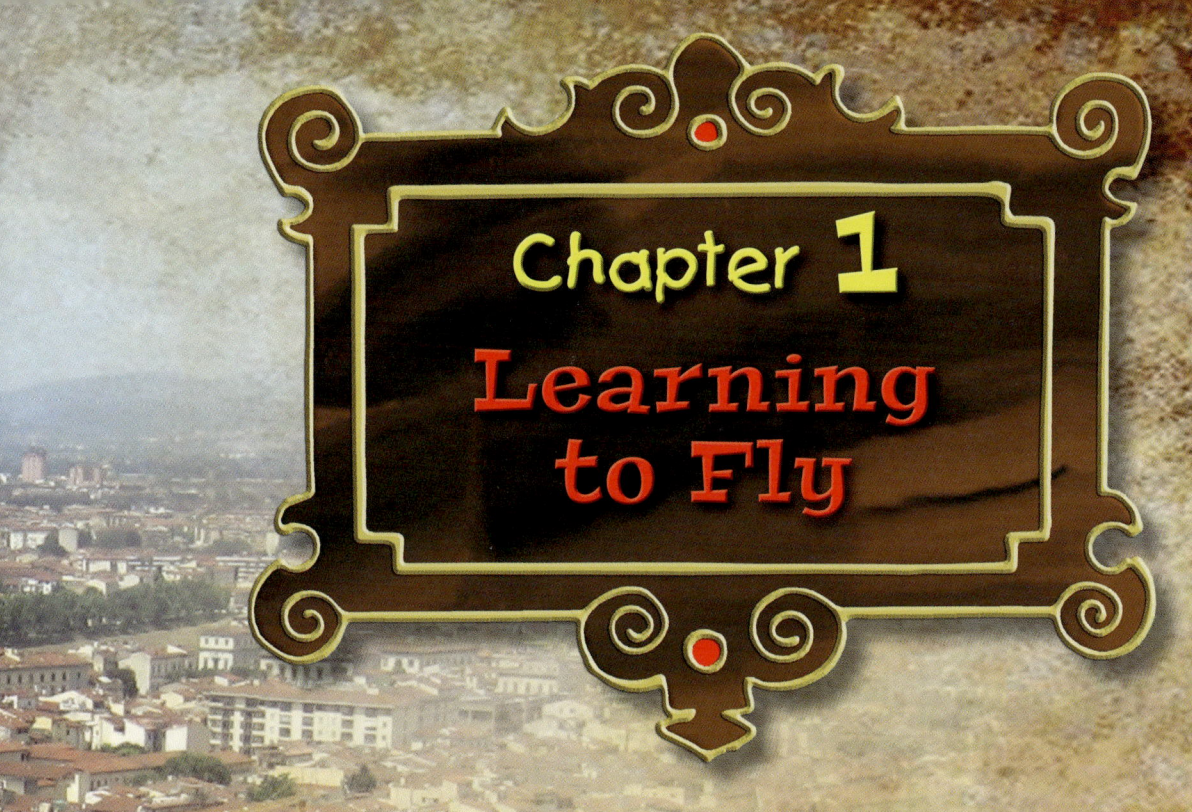

Chapter 1
Learning to Fly

I stood on top of the highest bell tower in Florence, Italy. People looked like ants as I peered down on them from Giotto's campanile **(kam-pah-NEE-lee)** 277 feet in the sky. The warm summer breeze blew across my face, bringing the smells of the Italian countryside to my young nose. I felt peaceful and happy.

Just then, a voice behind me asked, "Bartolomeo, are you going to jump or not?"

Leonardo watched how bats and birds fly to help him design his flying machine.

I turned to see my master, Leonardo da Vinci **(lee-uh-NAR-do dah VIN-chee)**, tapping his foot impatiently, waiting for me to jump.

"Are you sure these wings will work?" I pointed to the pair of giant wings on my back. My master had invented them after studying the flight of birds and bats. He believed his wings could allow a person to fly. I usually loved to help my master try out his inventions, but this one made me nervous.

"Come, come, Bartolomeo. I have done all the calculations **(kal-kyoo-LAY-shuns)** and they show these wings will easily allow a 50-pound boy to fly."

"But, Master Leonardo," I said, "I weigh 60 pounds."

My master looked confused. He pulled a piece of charcoal from his pocket and quickly did some math on the wall of the bell tower.

"Hmm ... okay, you'd better come down. You will surely die if you jump."

My master was a brilliant scientist, inventor, architect, musician, sculptor, and painter, but he was also a bit of a scatterbrain.

Leonardo's chalk self-portrait was drawn in 1512, when he was 50 years old.

Florence was the first city in Europe to have paved streets. It was also where the piano was invented.

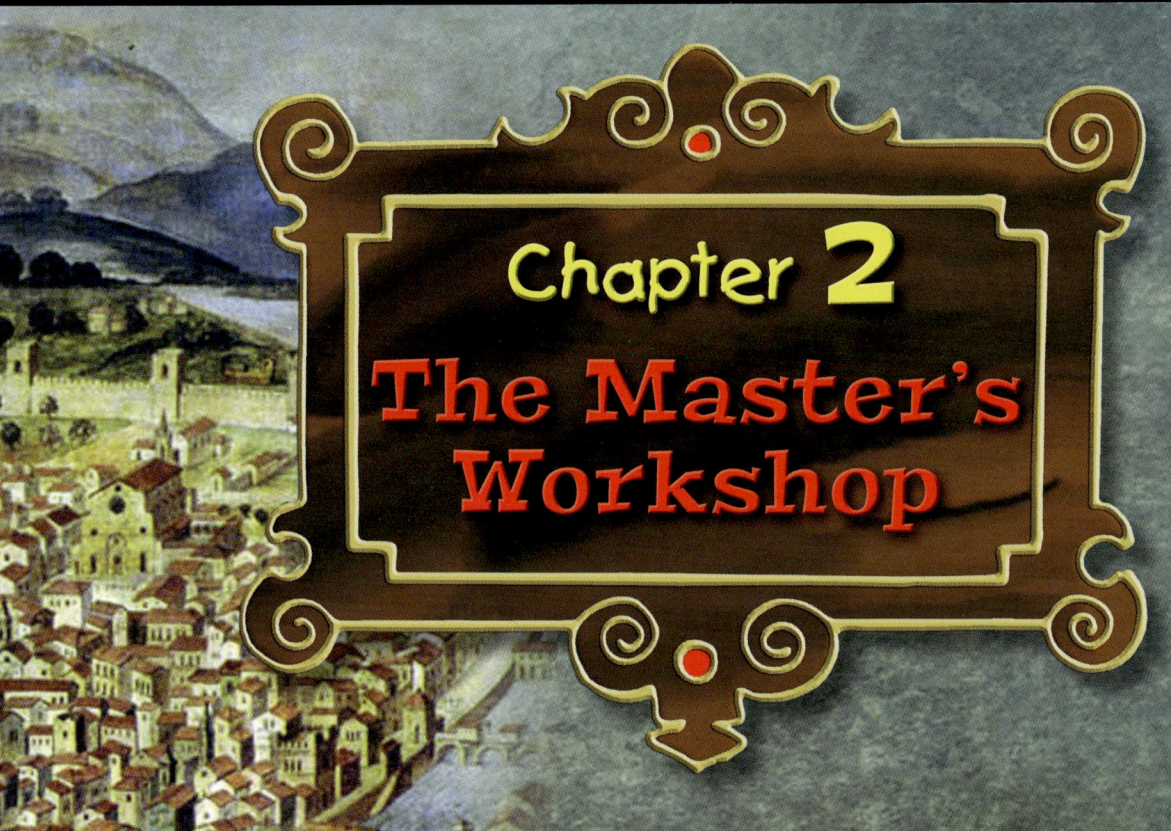

Chapter 2
The Master's Workshop

The year was 1503 during the era called the Renaissance **(REH-neh-zantz)**. It was a time of many new ideas in art and science. At ten years old, I was the apprentice **(uh-PREN-tis)** to one of the greatest geniuses the world had ever known.

I loved walking through his messy workroom. The walls were covered with drawings of the human body. There were portraits of beautiful women, and hand-drawn maps of Italy and Europe. There were even sketches for paintings he planned to paint.

Portraits and designs by Leonardo

On another wall were designs for his other inventions: a vehicle that could travel under water (Yeah, right!), a carriage with wheels that propelled itself (No horse? No way!), and something called a parachute **(PAH-ruh-shoot)** that would allow a person to survive a jump from a great height (Bet I will have to test that).

The Virgin of the Rocks (London)

I asked him once what he hoped to do with all these drawings and plans.

He answered, "I wish to work miracles."

Leonardo da Vinci always seemed to be doing five things at once, but he never seemed to finish any of them. It really annoyed the people who paid him for his work.

"All that bell tower climbing has made me hungry," Leonardo declared. "I need you to go to the market for some food." He wrote a list of items for me to buy: grapes, corn, mushrooms, peas, and grain.

He added, "Even though I don't eat meat, get yourself some beef." My master was always examining humans and animals to see how they worked, but he would not kill even a flea.

He handed me the grocery list. Leonardo was ambidextrous **(am-bee-DEKS-trus)**, meaning he could use his left and right hands equally well. Plus, he wrote backward, so the only way for me to read his list was to hold it up to a mirror. It made getting his groceries very hard.

Such was life working for Leonardo da Vinci.

The Baptism of Christ, 1472-1475

Chapter 3
The Young Genius

As I walked through the bustling city of Florence to the market, I thought about my master. I knew he was born in 1452 in the nearby town of Vinci. (His name means "Leonardo from Vinci.") His parents never married, and he ended up with 17 half-brothers and sisters!

As a young man, he showed talent as an artist. When Leonardo was around 14, he was sent to Florence to become an apprentice to the famous artist Andrea del Verrocchio **(on-DRAY-uh del vuh-ROH-kee-oh)**. There he mastered many artistic skills, including sculpting, drafting, drawing, painting, and model making.

One story says that while Verrocchio was working on a painting called *The Baptism* **(BAP-tiz-em)** *of Christ,* he asked Leonardo to

help him by painting a small angel. After he saw Leonardo's finished angel, Verrocchio swore he would never paint again — because his apprentice was a much better painter than he. I don't know if the story is true, but there is no doubt that Leonardo impressed his master very much.

The Annunciation

When Leonardo turned 20, he was named a master artist and was invited to join the painters' guild. He stayed with Verrocchio for many more years. Then he struck out on his own and moved to Milan, about 190 miles northwest of Florence.

The fresco *The Last Supper* in Milan, Italy

When I returned with the groceries, I found Leonardo staring at a particular drawing. He was lost in thought. I recognized the drawing immediately; It was a plan for a fresco, *The Last Supper.*

A fresco is a special kind of painting on a wall or ceiling, and this one was on the wall of Santa Maria delle Grazie Church. *The Last*

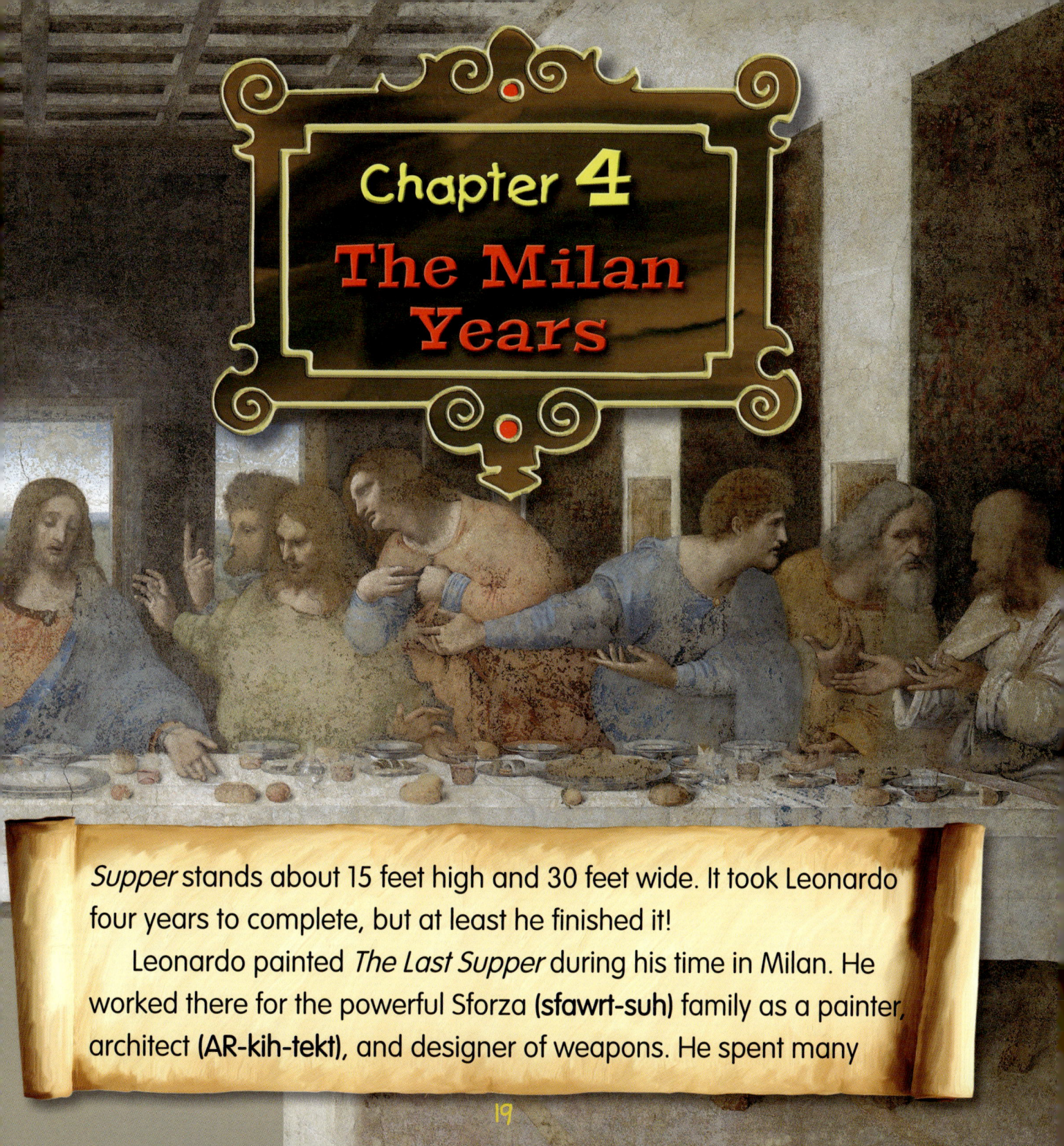

Chapter 4
The Milan Years

Supper stands about 15 feet high and 30 feet wide. It took Leonardo four years to complete, but at least he finished it!

Leonardo painted *The Last Supper* during his time in Milan. He worked there for the powerful Sforza **(sfawrt-suh)** family as a painter, architect **(AR-kih-tekt)**, and designer of weapons. He spent many

years working on a giant bronze horse statue for the Sforzas, but, no surprise, he never finished it.

When the Sforzas fell from power, Leonardo left Milan. After 17 years away, he returned to Florence. He brought all his secret notebooks that were full of ideas, drawings, and observations. He was always making scientific drawings. He especially loved to draw horses.

Whenever I could, I would sneak a look inside these magical notebooks. My favorite drawing was called *Vitruvian* **(vi-TROO-vee-un)** *Man*. To me it looked like a man doing jumping jacks, but Leonardo told me it was inspired by the great ancient Roman architect Vitruvius, who studied how the human body was put together.

My master believed that understanding how the body and the world worked made him a better artist. He once told me, "The painter's mind must . . . enter into nature's mind."

Suddenly, Leonardo, who had been lost in thought, jumped up. "Okay, Bartolomeo, gather my paints. We have a very important painting to do at a house you know well."

"Whose house?" I asked.

"Yours, of course!" said Leonardo.

Leonardo's sketches of animals and his famous *Vitruvian Man*

Chapter 5
My Stepmother, Lisa

I lived in a pretty nice neighborhood in Florence. My father was a successful silk merchant. My mother died when I was little, and my father had remarried. His wife, Lisa, had just given birth to my second stepbrother, Andrea. My father had hired Leonardo to paint my stepmother's portrait in our new house.

When we got there, I introduced my stepmother to Leonardo. She gave him one of her sweet smiles and sat down by the window to be painted. My father would come in every so often to see how the painting looked.

Of course, my father never received the painting. Leonardo spent fours years working on it, and still didn't finish. He would work for a while, but then he would put the painting aside for a very long time.

In the years that followed, even though my stepmother had grown old, I could still look at her portrait as it sat unfinished in Leonardo's studio and remember when she was young and beautiful. Whenever I looked at the painting called *Mona Lisa*, I remembered something Leonardo had once told me. He said, "What is fair in men passes away, but not so in art."

I wasn't sure what he meant at the time, but looking at *Mona Lisa*, I now understood: People and things can grow old and become less beautiful, but art is beautiful forever.

In 1519, when Leonardo was an old man and I was married with children, he sent for me. He showed me the painting of my stepmother. In my opinion, he never really stopped working on it, but the beautiful work of art he started when I was just a boy finally looked finished. Sadly, my friend Leonardo da Vinci died later that year.

St. John the Baptist was one of Leonardo's last paintings.

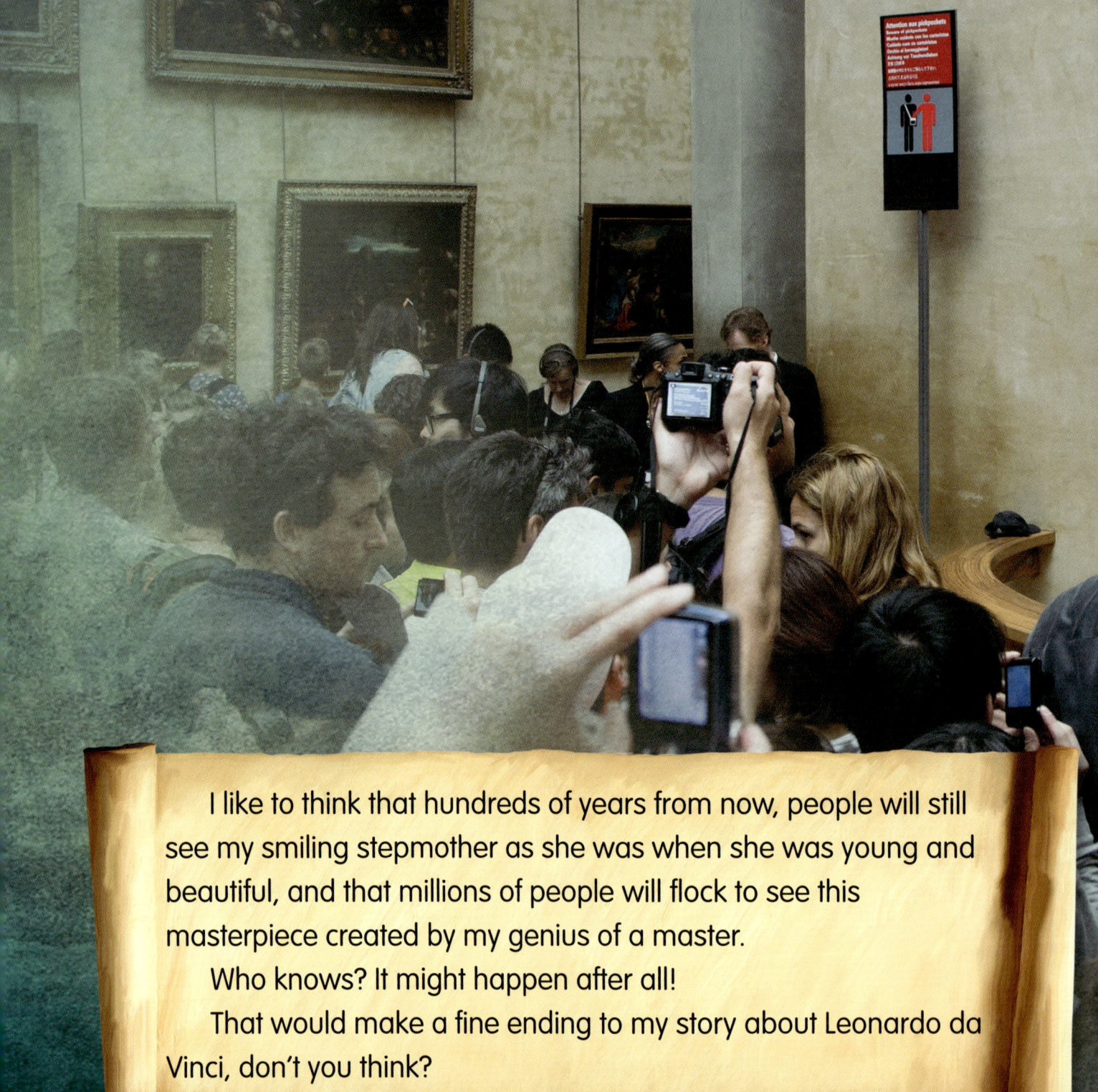

I like to think that hundreds of years from now, people will still see my smiling stepmother as she was when she was young and beautiful, and that millions of people will flock to see this masterpiece created by my genius of a master.

Who knows? It might happen after all!

That would make a fine ending to my story about Leonardo da Vinci, don't you think?

The *Mona Lisa* hangs in the Louvre museum in Paris, where she is visited by millions of people every year.

Timeline

1452 — Leonardo is born on April 15 to Ser Piero (a notary) and Caterina (a peasant girl).

1467–1477 — Leonardo is apprentice to painter Andrea del Verrocchio.

1482 — Leonardo begins serving the Duke of Milan, Ludovico Sforza.

1490–1495 — Leonardo keeps detailed notebooks of scientific thoughts and inventions.

1499 — The Duke of Milan falls from power. Leonardo leaves Milan.

1503 — Leonardo begins painting *Mona Lisa*.

1513–1516 — Leonardo works in Rome. His patron is Giuliano de Medici, whose family is very powerful.

1516 — Leonardo becomes the Premier Painter and Engineer and Architect of the King (Francis I of France).

1519 — Leonardo dies on May 2 in France.

Selected Works

1472	The Baptism of Christ	**1490**	Vitruvian Man
1472–1475	Annunciation	**1491**	The Virgin of the Rocks (London)
1473	Arno Valley	**1495**	The Last Supper
1474	Ginevra de' Benci	**1503**	Mona Lisa
1480	St. Jerome in the Wilderness	**1508**	Horse and Rider (sculpture)
1481	Adoration of the Magi	**1512**	Self-Portrait
1483	The Virgin of the Rocks (Paris)	**1513**	St. John the Baptist
1489–1490	Lady with an Ermine		

Arno Valley

Further Reading

Books

Esbaum, Jill. *National Geographic Little Kids First Big Book of Who* (National Geographic Little Kids First Big Books). Washington, DC: National Geographic Children's Books, 2015.

Knapp, Ruth. *Who Stole Mona Lisa*. New York: Bloomsbury, 2010.

Wurge, B.B. *The Last Notebook of Leonardo*. Massachusetts: Leapfrog Press, 2010.

Works Consulted

Atalay, Bulent, and Keith Wamsley. *Leonardo's Universe: The Renaissance World of Leonardo da Vinci*. Washington, D.C.: National Geographic, 2008.

Clayton, Martin, and Ron Philo. *Leonardo da Vinci, Anatomist*. London: Royal Collection Publications, 2012.

Feinberg, Larry. *The Young Leonardo: Art and Life in Fifteenth-Century Florence*. Cambridge: Cambridge University Press, 2011.

FitzRoy, Charles. *Renaissance Florence on 5 Florins a Day*. London: Thames & Hudson, 2010.

King, Ross. *Leonardo and the Last Supper*. New York: Bloomsburg, 2012.

Leonardo da Vinci. *The da Vinci Notebooks: A Dazzling Array of da Vinci's Celebrated and Inspirational Inventions, Theories, and Observations*. Ed. Emma Dickens. New York: Arcade Publishing, 2011.

Leonardo da Vinci. *Leonardo's Notebooks: Writing and Art of the Great Master*. Ed. H. Anna Suh. New York: Black Dog & Leventhal Publishers, 2013.

Lester, Toby. *Da Vinci's Ghost: Genius, Obsession, and How Leonardo Created the World in His Own Image*. New York: Free Press, 2012.

PBS: http://www.pbs.org/treasuresoftheworld/mona_lisa/mlevel_1/mtimeline.html

Tucker, Rebecca, and Paul Crenshaw. *Discovering Leonardo: The Art Lover's Guide to Understanding Leonardo da Vinci's Masterpieces*. New York: Universe Publishing, 2011.

On the Internet

Artsy Crafty Mom
  http://artsycraftsymom.com/leonardo-da-vinci-projects-for-kids/

Italia Kids
  http://www.italiakids.com/florence/

Kids Discover
  https://online.kidsdiscover.com/unit/renaissance

Glossary

ambidextrous (am-bee-DEKS-trus)—Able to write equally well with one's left or right hand.

apprentice (uh-PREN-tis)—A job in which a young person learns a skill from a master while working for little money.

architect (AR-kih-tekt)—Someone who designs buildings and oversees their construction.

calculations (kal-kyoo-LAY-shuns)—Math problems.

campanile (kam-puh-NEE-lee)—A tall, freestanding bell tower located near a church.

drafting (DRAF-ting)—Creating an early version of a project.

fresco (FRES-koh)—A painting that is done on the wet, plaster surface of a wall or ceiling, which then dries into a permanent work of art.

guild (GILD)—A powerful group made up of people with similar jobs or skills.

masterpiece (MAS-ter-pees)—An especially great piece of created work, such as a painting or sculpture.

portrait (POR-tret)—A drawing or photo that usually shows just a person's head and shoulders.

Renaissance (REH-neh-zantz)—The time between the 14th and 17th centuries when art, science, and literature prospered, especially in Italy.

sketch (SKECH)—A rough or unfinished drawing that is often the basis for a more complete work of art.

PHOTO CREDITS: p. 4—J. Miers; p. 4—Slashvee; p. 26—Victor Grigas; All other photos—Public Domain. Every measure has been taken to find all copyright holders of material used in this book. In the event any mistakes or omissions have happened within, attempts to correct them will be made in future editions of the book.

Index

ambidextrous   13

apprentice   9, 15, 16

Baptism of Christ, The   14, 15

drafting   15

drawing   10, 13, 15, 18, 21

Europe   8, 10

Florence (Italy)   4, 5, 8, 15, 17, 21, 23

Fresco   18

Giotto's campanile   4, 5

guild   17

inventions   6, 11

Italy   5, 10, 18

Last Supper, The   18, 19

Milan (Italy)   17, 18, 19, 21

model making   15

Mona Lisa   22, 24, 27

notebooks   21

painting   10, 15, 16, 18, 21, 23, 24

parachute   11

portrait   7, 10, 11, 23, 24

Renaissance   9

Santa Maria delle Grazie Church   18

sculpting   15

Sforza   19, 21

studio   24

Verrocchio, Andrea del   15, 16, 17

Vinci (Italy)   15

Vitruvian Man   21

Vitruvius   21